Easy Roasted Chicken Cookbook

50 Delicious Roasted Chicken Recipes

By
BookSumo Press
All rights reserved

Published by
http://www.booksumo.com

Table of Contents

Fall-Spice Chicken Roast 5

Hot and Sweet Chicken Roast 6

Baked Golden Chicken and Potato 7

How to Roast a Chicken 8

Southern Italian Chicken Roast 9

4-Ingredient Chicken Roast 10

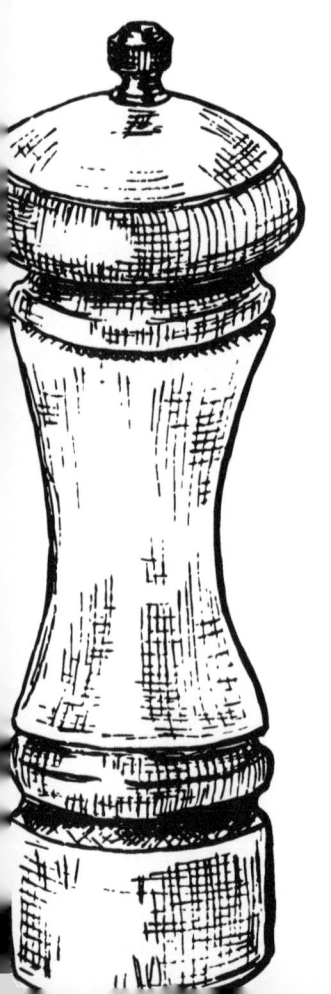

Herbs Marinade for Chicken Roast 11

Mediterranean Chicken Legs 12

Greek Inspired Chicken Roast 13

Glazed Chicken Roast 14

Veggies and Chicken Skillet Roast 15

Orangy Baked Chicken 16

Lemon & Thyme Chicken Roast 17

Country Chicken Roast Gravy 18

Paprika Chicken Roast 19

Chicken Roast Flavored Broccoli Roast 20

Spring Sage Chicken Roast 21

Spicy Lime Chicken Roast 22

Chipotle Chicken Barbecue 23

5-Ingredient Chicken Roast 24

French Rosemary Chicken Roast 25

Chicken Curry Roast 26

Cayenne Chicken Roast 27

Sweet and Salty Chicken Roast 28

Herbed Veggies and Chicken Roast 29

Doubled Virgin Chicken Roast 30

Lemon Pepper Chicken Roast 31

Nothing but Crisp Chicken Roast 32

Key Lime Glazed Honey Chicken 33

Fancy Rose's Chicken Bake 34

Baked Chicken with Italian Seasoning 36

Sweet Apricot Chicken Broth Roast 37

Nutty Chicken Curry Roast 38

Zesty Chicken Bake 39

Chicken Roast with Orange Sauce 40

Sweet Cinnamon Chicken Roast 41

Skin Stuffed Roasted Chicken Breasts 42

Bay's Chicken Roast 43

Soy sauce Chicken Bake 44

Basil Baked Chicken 45

Brown Chicken Roast 46

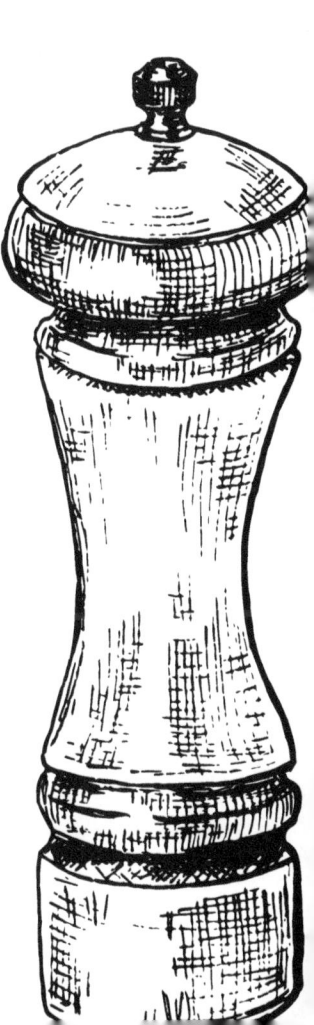

Plantain Chicken Roast 47

Sweet Veggies and Chicken Drumsticks Roast 48

Glazed Honey Veggies and Chicken Roast 49

Roasted Chicken Pot 50

Dijon Chicken Roast 51

Sweet and Tangy Baked Chicken 52

Baked Tahini Hummus 53

Jamaican Wings Roast 54

Fall-Spice Chicken Roast

Prep Time: 15 mins
Total Time: 1 d 1 h 35 m

Servings per Recipe: 6
Calories   387 kcal
Fat   22.8 g
Carbohydrates   1.6 g
Protein   41 g
Cholesterol   129 mg
Sodium   900 mg

Ingredients

- 2 tsp salt
- 1 tsp white sugar
- 1/8 tsp ground cloves
- 1/8 tsp ground allspice
- 1/8 tsp brown sugar
- 1/8 tsp ground cinnamon
- 1 (4 lb) whole chicken
- 5 cloves garlic, crushed

Directions

1. Get a small mixing bowl: Mix in it the salt, sugar, cloves, allspice, brown sugar, and cinnamon to make the rub. Massage the rub into the chicken and place it in the fridge for a whole 24 h day.
2. Before you do anything set the oven to 500 F.
3. Place the garlic and inside of the chicken and place it with its breast facing down in a roasting pan.
4. Cook in the oven for 17 min. Lower the oven heat to 450 F and cook the chicken for another 17 min.
5. Baste the chicken with the fat and dripping that gathered in the roasting pan. Once again reduce the oven heat to 425 F and cook the chicken for 32 min.
6. Cover the chicken with a piece of foil and let it rest for 22 min then serve it.
7. Enjoy.

HOT AND SWEET
Chicken Roast

🥣 Prep Time: 15 mins
🕒 Total Time: 1 hr 25 mins

Servings per Recipe: 6
Calories 558 kcal
Fat 26.8 g
Carbohydrates 37.1g
Protein 41.2 g
Cholesterol 140 mg
Sodium 225 mg

Ingredients

1 (4 lb) whole chicken, cut lengthwise
kosher salt to taste
freshly ground black pepper
1 tsp ground cinnamon, or as needed
1 C. water
1 C. maple syrup

1 lemon, juiced
2 chile peppers, chopped
2 tbsp butter, melted

Directions

1. Before you do anything set the oven to 375 F.
2. Season the chicken with cinnamon, salt and pepper. Pour the water in a broiler pan and place the chicken in it then cook it for 35 min.
3. Get a small bowl: Mix in it the maple syrup, lemon juice, and chile peppers. Pour the mix all over the chicken and cook it for 38 min.
4. Drain the chicken from the drippings and lay on it the butter then roast it in the oven for 14 min. Serve it warm.
5. Enjoy.

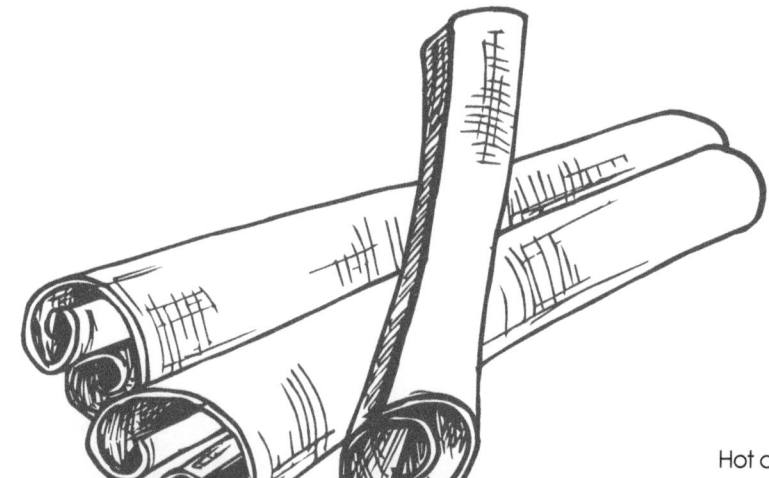

Baked Golden Chicken and Potato

Prep Time: 30 mins
Total Time: 1 hr 40 mins

Servings per Recipe: 6
Calories   423 kcal
Fat   18.9 g
Carbohydrates   33.8g
Protein   28.7 g
Cholesterol   81 mg
Sodium   161 mg

Ingredients

- 1 serving cooking spray
- 2 sweet potatoes, sliced very thinly
- 2 Yukon Gold potatoes, sliced
- 1 large onion, sliced
- 1 (2 to 3 lb) roasting chicken
- 2 tbsp olive oil, or to taste
- 1 pinch salt and ground black pepper to taste

Directions

1. Before you do anything set the oven to 400 F. Spray some cooking spray on a roasting pan and place it aside.
2. Place the sweet potato slices followed by golden potato and onion in the roasting pan.
3. Put the chicken on top with its breast facing down. Make a large cut alone the chicken backbone and remove it then press it open in the shape of a butterfly.
4. Drizzle the olive oil on the chicken and sprinkle on it some salt and pepper then place it with the breast facing down on the veggies.
5. Cook the chicken and potato in the oven for 1 h 10 min. Allow the potato and chicken roast to rest for 12 min then serve them warm.
6. Enjoy.

HOW TO ROAST
a Chicken

🥣 Prep Time: 10 mins
🕒 Total Time: 1 hr 40 mins

Servings per Recipe: 6
Calories	423 kcal
Fat	32.1 g
Carbohydrates	1.2g
Protein	30.9 g
Cholesterol	97 mg
Sodium	662 mg

Ingredients

1 (3 lb) whole chicken, giblets removed
salt and black pepper to taste
1 tbsp onion powder, or to taste
1/2 C. margarine, divided
1 stalk celery, leaves removed

Directions

1. Before you do anything set the oven to 350 F.
2. Season the whole chicken with some salt and pepper. Season its inside with onion powder and place in it 3 tbsp of margarine.
3. Place the whole chicken in a large roasting pan and place the remaining margarine on it in the shape of dollops. Chop the celery into pieces and place them in the middle of the chicken.
4. Place the chicken in the oven and roast it for 1 h 20 min. Baste the chicken with the fat and melted margarine that pooled around whole cooking.
5. Place a large piece of foil over the chicken and allow it to rest for 35 min. Serve it warm.
6. Enjoy.

Southern Italian Chicken Roast

Prep Time: 15 mins
Total Time: 1 hr 45 mins

Servings per Recipe: 8
Calories	405 kcal
Fat	29.2 g
Carbohydrates	3.6 g
Protein	32.2 g
Cholesterol	128 mg
Sodium	178 mg

Ingredients

- 2 tsp Italian seasoning
- 1/2 tsp seasoning salt
- 1/2 tsp mustard powder
- 1 tsp garlic powder
- 1/2 tsp ground black pepper
- 1 (3 lb) whole chicken
- 2 lemons
- 2 tbsp olive oil

Directions

1. Before you do anything set the oven to 350 F.
2. Get a small bowl: Mix in it the mustard powder with garlic powder, a pinch of salt and pepper to make the rub.
3. Massage the rub into the chicken from using 1 1/2 tsp for the inside and the remaining seasoning for the outside.
4. Get a small mixing bowl: Mix in it the olive oil with the juice of 2 lemons then pour it all over the chicken.
5. Roast the chicken in the oven for 1 h 32 min while basting it with the drippings from the pan every 30 min. Allow the roast to rest for 15 min then serve it.
6. Enjoy.

4-INGREDIENT
Chicken Roast

Prep Time: 10 mins
Total Time: 2 hrs 10 mins

Servings per Recipe: 6
Calories   291 kcal
Fat   17.2 g
Carbohydrates   1.3g
Protein   30.8 g
Cholesterol   97 mg
Sodium   94 mg

Ingredients

1 (3 lb) whole chicken, rinsed
salt and pepper to taste
1 small onion, quartered

1/4 C. chopped fresh rosemary

Directions

1. Before you do anything set the oven to 350 F.
2. Sprinkle some salt and pepper on the whole chicken then place the rosemary with onion in its cavity.
3. Place the chicken in a large roasting pan and cook it in the oven for 2 h 32 min. Allow the chicken to rest for 15 to 20 min then serve it.
4. Enjoy.

Herbs Marinade for Chicken Roast

Prep Time: 10 mins
Total Time: 10 mins

Servings per Recipe: 4
Calories   20 kcal
Fat   0.3 g
Carbohydrates   4.4 g
Protein   0.8 g
Cholesterol   0 mg
Sodium   977 mg

Ingredients

1 tbsp celery flakes
1 tbsp kosher salt
1 tbsp paprika
1 tbsp garlic powder
1 tbsp onion powder
1 tbsp ground thyme
2 tsp dried sage
1 1/2 tsp ground black pepper
1 1/2 tsp dried rosemary
1/2 tsp cayenne pepper

Directions

1. Get a small bowl: Combine it all the ingredients and whisk them well.
2. Get a food processor: Transfer the mix to it and blend them smooth. Massage the marinade with some olive oil to the chicken and roasted the way you like.
3. Enjoy.

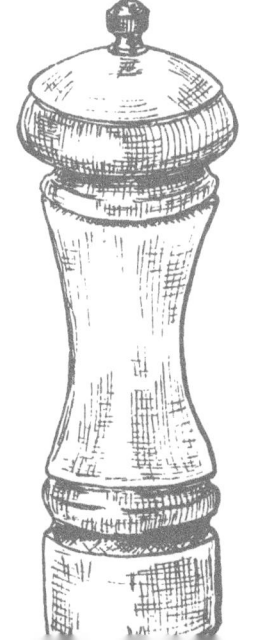

MEDITERRANEAN
Chicken Legs

Prep Time: 10 mins
Total Time: 1 hr 25 mins

Servings per Recipe: 4
Calories	516 kcal
Fat	34.6 g
Carbohydrates	16.8g
Protein	41.9 g
Cholesterol	140 mg
Sodium	2464 mg

Ingredients

- 4 chicken leg quarters, with bone and skin
- 1/4 C. olive oil
- 4 lemons, halved
- 4 tsp dried oregano
- 4 tsp dried basil
- 4 tsp garlic powder
- 4 tsp salt
- 4 tsp ground black pepper

Directions

1. Before you do anything set the oven to 350 F.
2. Coat each chicken quarter with 1 tbsp of olive oil then drizzle the lemon juice of 2 lemons all over them.
3. Place the chicken quarters in a large roasting pan and put the lemon halves beside them.
4. Get a small mixing bowl: Mix in it the oregano with garlic powder, basil, a pinch of salt and pepper then sprinkle the mix all over the chicken legs equally.
5. Roast the chicken legs for 1 h 20 min while basting them with the drippings every once in a while then serve them warm.
6. Enjoy.

Greek Inspired Chicken Roast

Prep Time: 15 mins
Total Time: 1 hr

Servings per Recipe: 6
Calories   546 kcal
Fat   34.5 g
Carbohydrates   5.4 g
Protein   52 g
Cholesterol   205 mg
Sodium   347 mg

Ingredients

1 whole chicken, cut into 8 pieces
1 onion, cut into wedges
1 lemon, sliced
8 cloves garlic
4 sprigs fresh rosemary
1/4 C. olive oil
1/2 tsp salt

1/2 tsp ground black pepper

Directions

1. Before you do anything set the oven to 450 F.
2. Get a large bowl: Stir in the lemon slices with garlic, rosemary, chicken and onion then pour the oil all over them and stir them.
3. Season them with some salt and pepper then stir them again.
4. Lay the chicken pieces in a large roasting pan and cook them for 48 min. Allow them to rest for 10 min then serve them warm.
5. Enjoy.

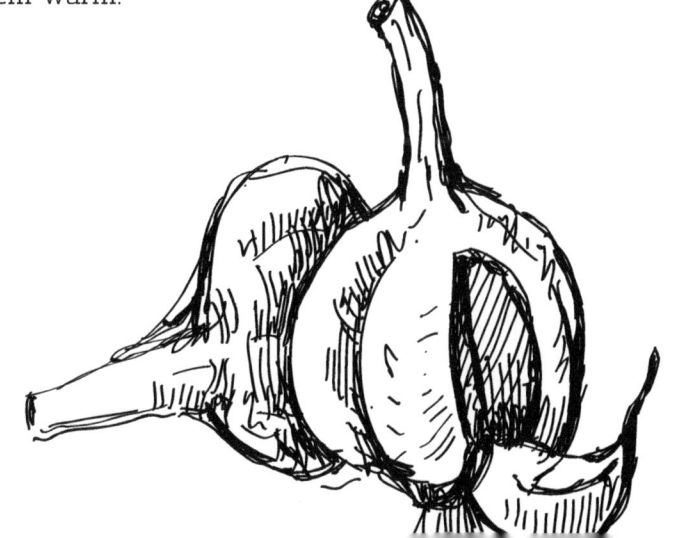

GLAZED
Chicken Roast

Prep Time: 15 mins
Total Time: 1 hr 55 mins

Servings per Recipe: 8
Calories	469 kcal
Fat	26 g
Carbohydrates	10g
Protein	46.4 g
Cholesterol	145 mg
Sodium	836 mg

Ingredients

2 (3 lb) whole chickens, quartered
Chicken Spice Rub:
1 tbsp brown sugar
1 tbsp sea salt
1 1/2 tsp garlic powder
1 1/2 tsp onion powder
1 1/2 tsp paprika
1 tsp dried oregano
1/2 tsp dry mustard
1/2 tsp celery seed
1/4 tsp cayenne pepper
Glaze:
1/4 C. maple syrup
1 tbsp yellow mustard
1 1/2 tsp spicy brown mustard
1/2 tsp garlic powder
1/2 tsp onion powder
1/2 tsp paprika
1/4 tsp ground black pepper

Directions

1. Get a small bowl: Mix in it the sugar, sea salt, 1 1/2 tsp garlic powder, 1 1/2 tsp onion powder, 1 1/2 tsp paprika, oregano, dry mustard, celery seed, and cayenne pepper.
2. Massage the spices mix into the chicken pieces and place them in a plastic wrap and place them in the fridge for 1 h to absorb the flavors.
3. To make the glaze: Get a small bowl and mix in it the maple syrup, yellow mustard, brown mustard, 1/2 tsp garlic powder, 1/2 tsp onion powder, 1/2 tsp paprika, and black pepper.
4. Before you do anything set the oven to 425 F.
5. Place the breasts pieces in the middles and place the remaining chicken pieces on the sides then cook them in the oven for 17 min.
6. Brush the chicken pieces with the glaze then cook them for another 17 min. Brush the chicken pieces again and cook them for 12 to 14 min or until it the chicken is done.
7. Serve your roasted glazed chicken.
8. Enjoy.

Veggies and Chicken Skillet Roast

Prep Time: 15 mins
Total Time: 1 hr 5 mins

Servings per Recipe: 2
Calories   601 kcal
Fat   23.7 g
Carbohydrates   45.8g
Protein   50.4 g
Cholesterol   157 mg
Sodium   407 mg

Ingredients

- 1/4 C. unsalted butter
- 2 bone-in skin-on chicken breasts
- 4 potatoes, peeled and cut into 1-inch cubes
- 4 carrots, peeled and cut into 1/2-inch rounds
- 3 stalks celery, cut into 1/2-inch slices
- 1 tbsp fresh rosemary
- 1 tsp fresh lemon thyme leaves
- 1/2 tsp smoked paprika
- 1/2 tsp garlic powder
- 1/2 tsp seasoned salt
- 1/4 tsp ground white pepper
- salt and ground black pepper to taste

Directions

1. Place a large pan over medium heat and cook in it the butter until it melts. Add the chicken with its skin facing down and cook it for 6 min.
2. Turn it and place around it the veggies. Finley chop the herbs and sprinkle them on top. Sprinkle the paprika with garlic powder, a pinch of salt and pepper on top then put on the lid.
3. Cook the roast for 48 min until the chicken is done then serve it warm.
4. Enjoy.

ORANGY
Baked Chicken

🥣 Prep Time: 10 mins
🕐 Total Time: 1 d 2 h 30 m

Servings per Recipe: 6
Calories	161 kcal
Fat	6.4 g
Carbohydrates	0.3g
Protein	24 g
Cholesterol	72 mg
Sodium	1816 mg

Ingredients

- 1 whole chicken
- 2 tbsp salt, or as needed
- 2 tsp grated orange zest
- 1 tsp dried rosemary
- 1 tsp dried thyme

Directions

1. Before you do anything set the oven to 350 F.
2. Get a small bowl: Mix in it the orange zest, rosemary, and thyme . Massage 3/4 of the mix into the chicken then place the remaining of it in the inside of the chicken.
3. Place a loose cover of plastic cover over the chicken then place in the fridge for 2 to days.
4. Place the chicken in a large roasting pan then cook it in the oven for 2 h 25 min. Place a sheet of foil over the chicken and place it aside to rest for 23 min then serve it.
5. Enjoy.

Lemon & Thyme Chicken Roast

Prep Time: 15 mins
Total Time: 2 hrs

Servings per Recipe: 6
Calories   450 kcal
Fat   26.9 g
Carbohydrates   4.5g
Protein   46.5 g
Cholesterol   145 mg
Sodium   221 mg

Ingredients

- 1 lemon, zested
- 2 sprigs fresh rosemary, chopped
- 3 sprigs fresh thyme, chopped
- 2 cloves garlic, minced
- 1 tsp olive oil
- 1 pinch sea salt and pepper to taste
- 1 (3 lb) whole chicken
- 4 whole garlic cloves

Directions

1. Before you do anything set the oven to 425 F.
2. Get a small bowl: Mix in it the lemon zest, rosemary, thyme, and minced garlic, olive oil, a pinch of salt and pepper.
3. Massage the marinade all over the chicken and rub it under the skin. Place half lemon inside the chicken with the garlic cloves.
4. Place the chicken in a large broiler pan and pour the juice of the remaining half lemon all over it. Roast it in the oven for 1 h 40 min.
5. Place a large piece of foil around the chicken and place it aside to rest for 12 min then serve it.
6. Enjoy.

COUNTRY Chicken Roast Gravy

Prep Time: 20 mins
Total Time: 40 mins

Servings per Recipe: 20
Calories	43 kcal
Fat	0.4 g
Carbohydrates	4.2g
Protein	5.8 g
Cholesterol	< 1 mg
Sodium	464 mg

Ingredients

- 1/4 C. drippings from a roast chicken
- 2 1/2 tbsp all-purpose flour
- 2 C. cold chicken stock, or more if needed
- salt and ground black pepper to taste

Directions

1. Drain the fats from the dripping of a chicken roast pan and place it aside. Add the flour to the pan and mix it well then add some of the fat if the mix is too dry.
2. Transfer the flour mix to a small saucepan over low heat and cook it until it becomes light brown in color for about 6 min.
3. Stir in 1/3 C. of stock into the mix while mixing all the time then keep repeating the process with the remaining stock until you add all of it
4. Cook the gravy until it starts simmering then keep cooking it for 9 min until it becomes creamy and thick.
5. Pour the grave through a fine sieve and strain then pour it back into the saucepan and heat it through then serve it warm.
6. Enjoy.

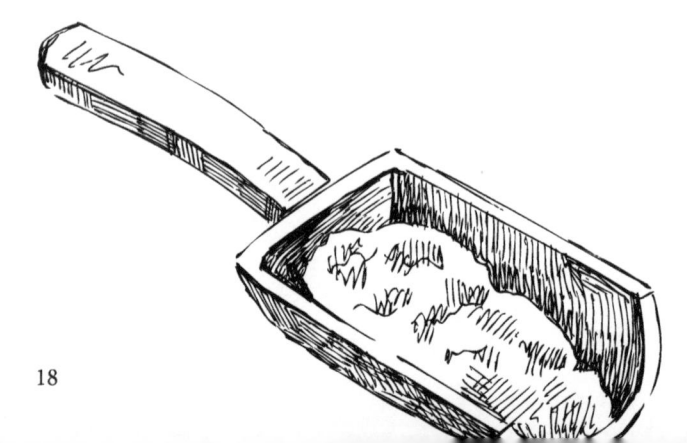

Paprika Chicken Roast

Prep Time: 15 mins
Total Time: 1 hr 15 mins

Servings per Recipe: 6
Calories   431 kcal
Fat   25.7 g
Carbohydrates   0.9 g
Protein   46.1 g
Cholesterol   146 mg
Sodium   528 mg

Ingredients

cooking spray
1 whole chicken, cut into 8 pieces
1 tsp salt
1 tsp ground black pepper
1 tsp ground paprika
1 tsp garlic powder
1 tsp dried oregano

Directions

1. Before you do anything set the oven to 425 F. Oil roasting pan and place it aside.
2. Place the chicken pieces in the pan then season them with paprika, garlic powder, oregano, a pinch of salt and pepper on both sides.
3. Cook the chicken in the oven for 1 h 5 min. Serve it warm.
4. Enjoy.

CHICKEN ROAST
Flavored Broccoli Roast

Prep Time: 5 mins
Total Time: 15 mins

Servings per Recipe: 4
Calories   143 kcal
Fat   13.1 g
Carbohydrates   5.5g
Protein   2.2 g
Cholesterol   13 mg
Sodium   25 mg

Ingredients

1/4 C. roast chicken drippings
1 head broccoli, cut into florets
2 cloves garlic, chopped

Directions

1. Right after roasting a chicken drain it from the drippings and place it aside. Keep the oven on.
2. Remove the most of the drippings until 1/4 C. of it is left. Add the garlic to the remaining drippings in the pan and garlic. Stir them well and cook them in the oven for 7 min.
3. Serve your roast warm.
4. Enjoy.

Spring Sage Chicken Roast

Prep Time: 15 mins
Total Time: 1 hr 15 mins

Servings per Recipe: 6
Calories	446 kcal
Fat	32.2 g
Carbohydrates	1.1g
Protein	36.2 g
Cholesterol	133 mg
Sodium	228 mg

Ingredients

1/4 C. lemon balm leaves, divided
1/4 C. fresh sage leaves, divided
1/4 C. softened butter
salt and pepper to taste
1 (3 1/2) lb whole chicken
1 tsp garlic powder
2 tbsp olive oil

Directions

1. Before you do anything set the oven to 400 F.
2. Reserve 1/3 of sage leaves and lemon balm leaves aside. Chop the rest of them finely.
3. Get a small bowl: Add to it the chopped sage and lemon leaves with butter, a pinch of salt and pepper. Mix them well and massage the mix into the chicken reaching under its skin.
4. Place remaining 1/3 of lemon leaves and sage inside the chicken then place it in a broiling pan with its chicken breast facing down.
5. Cook the chicken in the oven for 32 min then flip it and cook it for 22 min. Wrap the chicken in a piece of foil and let it rest for 12 min then serve it warm.
6. Enjoy.

SPICY Lime Chicken Roast

Prep Time: 15 mins
Total Time: 1 hr 45 mins

Servings per Recipe: 8
Calories   220 kcal
Fat   11 g
Carbohydrates   7.4g
Protein   19.9 g
Cholesterol   78 mg
Sodium   1173 mg

Ingredients

1/2 C. Sriracha chile sauce
1/4 C. soy sauce
1/4 C. white vinegar
1/4 C. lime juice
2 tbsp butter, melted
1 tbsp brown sugar, or more to taste
1 tbsp grated fresh ginger root

8 chicken thighs, or more to taste
cooking spray
2 tbsp chopped fresh cilantro
8 lime wedges

Directions

1. Before you do anything set the oven to 425 F. Grease a roasting pan.
2. Get a small bowl: Mix in it the chile sauce, soy sauce, white vinegar, lime juice, butter, brown sugar, and ginger to make the marinade.
3. Place the chicken thighs in a large zip lock bag then pour the marinade all over it. Seal the bag and shake it roughly then place it aside for 2 h to an overnight.
4. Drain the chicken thighs and place them in the roasting pan then cook them in oven for 22 min. Drizzle some of the remaining marinade on the chicken thighs and cook them for 14 min.
5. Serve your chicken thighs warm.
6. Enjoy.

Chipotle Chicken Barbecue

Prep Time: 20 mins
Total Time: 9 hrs 10 mins

Servings per Recipe: 6
Calories   217 kcal
Fat   4.2 g
Carbohydrates   19.2g
Protein   26.9 g
Cholesterol   67 mg
Sodium   293 mg

Ingredients

- 1/4 C. ground black pepper
- 2 tbsp smoked paprika
- 4 skinless, boneless chicken breast halves, lbed flat
- 2 tbsp ground chipotle
- 2 cubes vegetable bouillon, or more to taste
- 1/4 C. chopped fresh rosemary
- 16 baby carrots, chopped
- 2 shiitake mushrooms, sliced (optional)
- 2 stalks celery, chopped
- 5 cloves garlic, chopped
- 1 pinch ground chipotle, or to taste
- 1/4 C. barbeque sauce

Directions

1. Season the chicken breasts from one side with paprika and black pepper then rub them with 1 1/2 tsp of chipotle powder for each breast on the second side.
2. Transfer the chicken breasts to a large zip lock bag and place them in the fridge for 9 h.
3. Place a large pot of water with pinch of salt over medium heat and cook it until it starts boiling. Dissolve the bouillon in the hot water and add to it the rosemary.
4. Add the celery with mushroom, garlic, and carrot. Cook them for 12 min. Drain the veggies from the pot and place them aside.
5. Before you do anything preheat the grill to 300 F. Get a small bowl and fill it with water then soak in it 8 toothpicks.
6. Place the chicken breasts on a working area with the chipotle seasoned side facing down.
7. Divide cooked veggies between the chicken breasts and roll them around them then secure them with toothpicks. Cook the stuffed Chicken Breasts on the grill for 32 min. Smother the stuffed chicken breasts with the barbecue sauce and cook them for 12 min then serve them warm.
8. Enjoy.

5-INGREDIENT
Chicken Roast

🥣 Prep Time: 15 mins
🕐 Total Time: 1 hr 45 mins

Servings per Recipe: 6
Calories	388 kcal
Fat	22.9 g
Carbohydrates	3.1g
Protein	41.2 g
Cholesterol	129 mg
Sodium	319 mg

Ingredients

1 (4 lb) whole chicken
salt and pepper to taste
1 large lemon, sliced
6 cloves garlic, sliced
6 sprigs thyme

Directions

1. Before you do anything set the oven to 325 F. Line a roasting pan with large parchment paper.
2. Sprinkle some salt and pepper on the chicken. Place inside it half of the lemon slices.
3. Transfer it to the middle of the roasting pan with its breast facing up then lat on it the thyme sprigs with garlic slices.
4. Place the remaining lemon slices on top then wrap the parchment paper the chicken loosely.
5. Cook it in the oven for 1 h 45 min to 2 h then serve it warm.
6. Enjoy.

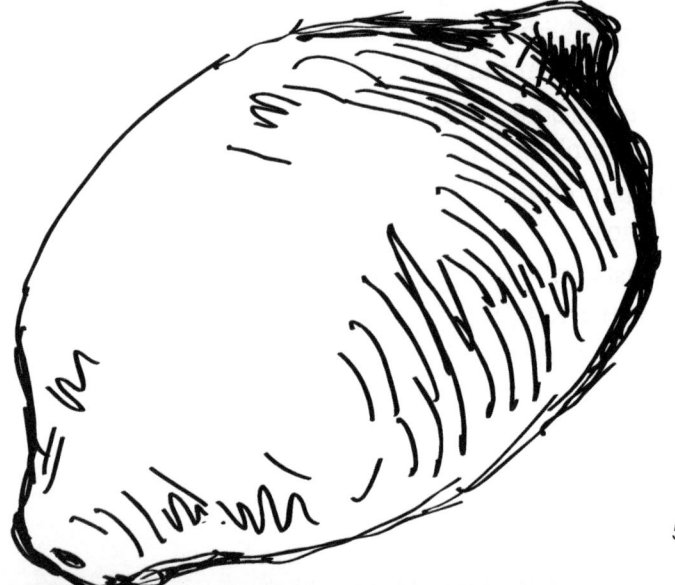

French Rosemary Chicken Roast

🥣 Prep Time: 20 mins
🕐 Total Time: 1 hr 55 mins

Servings per Recipe: 6
Calories	349 kcal
Fat	13.8 g
Carbohydrates	9.1g
Protein	44.2 g
Cholesterol	128 mg
Sodium	269 mg

Ingredients

- 1 (4 lb) whole chicken
- 1 tbsp olive oil, or as needed
- salt and ground black pepper to taste
- 1 large rosemary sprig, leaves stripped and finely chopped
- 1 large white onion, cut into 1-inch chunks
- 2 C. cubed French bread
- 1 large whole rosemary sprig
- 1/4 lemon, juiced

Directions

1. Before you do anything set the oven to 390 F. Grease a roasting pan.
2. Massage the oil into the chicken and season it with some salt. Massage the rosemary with black pepper into it as well.
3. Put the onion with bread inside the chicken and rosemary sprig. Transfer the chicken into a large skillet with the breast facing up and arrange the rest of the bread and onion around it.
4. Pour the lemon juice all over them. Cook the chicken in the oven for 32 min. Flip the chicken and cook it for another 32 min.
5. Allow the chicken to rest for 8 min then serve it.
6. Enjoy.

CHICKEN
Curry Roast

🥣 Prep Time: 15 mins
🕐 Total Time: 2 hrs 15 mins

Servings per Recipe: 6
Calories   409 kcal
Fat   25 g
Carbohydrates   2.2g
Protein   40.9 g
Cholesterol   129 mg
Sodium   269 mg

Ingredients

- 3 tbsp mild curry paste
- 1 tbsp olive oil
- 1 (4 lb) whole chicken
- 1 small onion, quartered

Directions

1. Before you do anything set the oven to 350 F.
2. Get a small bowl: Mix in it the olive oil with curry. Massage the mix into the chicken reaching under the skin and inside it. Stuff the chicken with onion and place it in a broiling pan.
3. Cook the chicken in the oven for 2 h 10 min. Serve your chicken warm.
4. Enjoy.

Cayenne Chicken Roast

Prep Time: 15 mins
Total Time: 5 hrs 25 mins

Servings per Recipe: 6
Calories   238
Fat   15.7 g
Cholesterol   71.3 mg
Sodium   1619.9 mg
Carbohydrates   6.2 g
Protein   17.6 g

Ingredients

- 4 tsp salt
- 2 tsp paprika
- 1 tsp cayenne pepper
- 1 tsp onion powder
- 1 tsp thyme
- 1 tsp white pepper
- 1/2 tsp garlic powder
- 1/2 tsp black pepper
- 1 large roasting chicken
- 2 large onions, peeled and quartered

Directions

1. Get a small bowl: Mix in it all the spices. Rub the whole chicken with the spice mix on the outside and inside and stuff it with onion.
2. Place the chicken in a large zip lock bag and place it in the fridge for an overnight.
3. Before you do anything set the oven to 250 F.
4. Transfer the chicken to a roasting pan and cook it in the oven for 5 h 10 min. Allow the chicken to rest for 10 min then serve it warm.
5. Enjoy.

SWEET and Salty Chicken Roast

Prep Time: 10 mins
Total Time: 3 hrs 10 mins

Servings per Recipe: 6
Calories 578.9
Fat 39.9 g
Cholesterol 187.5 mg
Sodium 1086 mg
Carbohydrates 4 g
Protein 48.3 g

Ingredients

1 1/2 kg chicken pieces (3 lb)
1/3 C. dark soy sauce
1 tbsp honey
1 tsp five-spice powder
1 tsp garlic (crushed)
1 tsp gingerroot (grated)
1 tbsp sesame oil

Directions

1. Before you do anything set the oven to 325 F.
2. Pat the chicken pieces dry. Get a small: mix in it the remaining ingredient to make the marinade.
3. Get a large mixing bowl: toss in it the chicken pieces with the marinade and place in it the fridge to marinate for 2 h 20 min.
4. Place the chicken pieces in a large roasting pan and cook it in the oven for 32 min. Flip the chicken and cook it for 27 min.
5. Serve your chicken warm.
6. Enjoy.

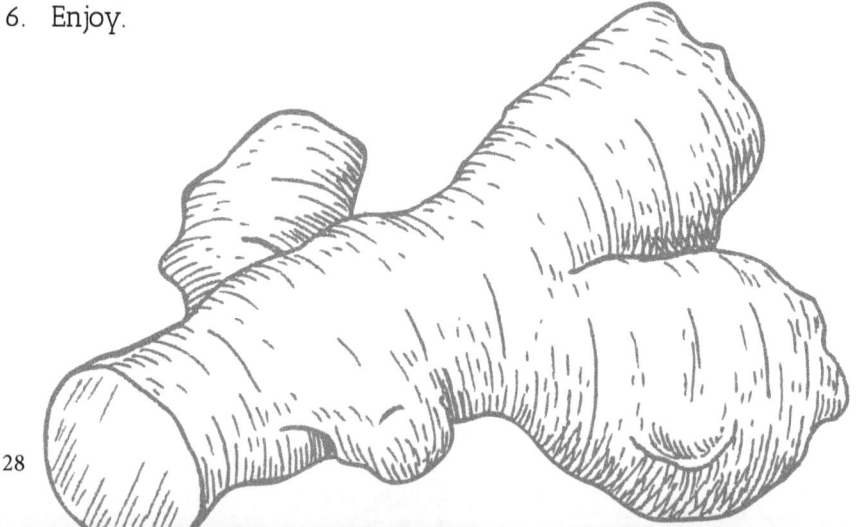

Herbed Veggies and Chicken Roast

Prep Time: 20 mins
Total Time: 1 hr 5 mins

Servings per Recipe: 4
Calories   352.9
Fat   11.8 g
Cholesterol   94.4 mg
Sodium   919.2 mg
Carbohydrates   34.7 g
Protein   28.4 g

Ingredients

- 1 1/2 lbs red potatoes, cut into 1 1/2-inch chunks
- 1 large onion, cut into wedges
- 4 garlic cloves
- 2 tbsp olive oil
- 1 1/4 tsp salt
- 1/2 tsp black pepper
- 1/2 tsp dried rosemary
- 1 lb boneless skinless chicken thighs, each cut in quarters
- 1 (10 oz) bag fresh spinach (remove stems)

Directions

1. Before you do anything set the oven to 475 F.
2. Toss the potatoes, onion, garlic, oil, salt, pepper and rosemary in a large broiling pan. Cook it in the oven for 14 min. Stir it and cook it for 12 min.
3. Season the chicken thighs with some salt and pepper. Add them to the veggies in the middle and coo it for 17 min.
4. Lay the spinach on top and cook them in the oven for 6 min. Serve your veggies and chicken roast warm.
5. Enjoy.

DOUBLED
Virgin Chicken Roast

Prep Time: 20 mins
Total Time: 2 hrs 5 mins

Servings per Recipe: 4
Calories	912.2
Fat	70.8 g
Cholesterol	270.4 mg
Sodium	241 mg
Carbohydrates	2.5 g
Protein	63.8 g

Ingredients

2 garlic cloves
kosher salt
1 lemon, halved and juiced, halves reserved
1 tsp rosemary
1 tsp sweet paprika
3/4 tsp ground cumin
1/2 tsp hot paprika
fresh ground pepper
1/4 C. extra virgin olive oil
1 (3 lb) chicken
2 tbsp unsalted butter, softened

Directions

1. Before you do anything set the oven to 350 F.
2. Mince the garlic and transfer it to a small bowl. Add 1 tsp of kosher salt and mix them well. Add the lemon juice, rosemary, sweet paprika, cumin, 1/2 tsp pepper, and olive oil.
3. Rub 1 tbsp of mix under the skin of the chicken without tearing it. Season the inside of the chicken with some salt and pepper.
4. Massage 1 tbsp of butter into the chicken's breast. Get a small bowl and mix in it the rest of the butter into the rest of the chicken with 1 tbsp of the spices mix.
5. Place the lemon halves inside the chicken and secure its legs with a kitchen string. Place the chicken in a large roasting pan and cook it for 1 h 32 min.
6. Allow the chicken to rest for 16 min. Strain the drippings of the chicken and heat them through in a small saucepan.
7. Serve your chicken with the heated drippings.
8. Enjoy.

Lemon Pepper Chicken Roast

Prep Time: 40 mins
Total Time: 2 hrs 10 mins

Servings per Recipe: 4
Calories   529.3
Fat   40.6 g
Cholesterol   175.7 mg
Sodium   14645.1 mg
Carbohydrates   0.8 g
Protein   37.9 g

Ingredients

1 (3 - 3 1/2 lb) roasting chickens
1/2 C. kosher salt
1 quart water
2 tbsp butter, melted
2 garlic cloves, minced
1 tsp dried basil, crushed
1/2 tsp salt
1/2 tsp ground sage
1/2 tsp dried thyme, crushed
1/4 tsp lemon-pepper seasoning or 1/4 tsp ground black pepper

Directions

1. Get a large zip lock bag and put the chicken on it. Sprinkle on it the kosher salt then pour the water on it. Close the bag and shake it slightly to make the brine.
2. Place the chicken bag in the fridge for 35 min. Drain the chicken from the brine and clean it with some cold water then dry it.
3. Before you do anything set the oven to 375 F.
4. Get a small bow: mix in it the herbs with lemon pepper and 1/2 tsp of salt to make the rub.
5. Get a small bowl: place in it the butter and melt it in a microwave. Add the minced garlic and mix them well.
6. Brush the back of the chicken with half of the butter mix then season it with half of the herbs mix. Flip the chicken and do the same to it.
7. Place the chicken in a roasting pan and cook it in the oven for 1 h 40 min. Serve it warm.
8. Enjoy.

NOTHING BUT CRISP
Chicken Roast

🥣 Prep Time: 10 mins
⏱ Total Time: 2 hrs 10 mins

Servings per Recipe: 4
Calories 782.6
Fat 61.9 g
Cholesterol 236.8 mg
Sodium 276.6 mg
Carbohydrates 3.1 g
Protein 50.7 g

Ingredients

4 lbs whole chickens
2 garlic cloves
3 tbsp butter
1 onion
2 tbsp vegetable oil
salt and pepper

Directions

1. Before you do anything set the oven to 325 F.
2. Dry the chicken. Pour 1 tbsp of on a paper towel and pat chicken with it then season it with some salt and pepper.
3. Place the garlic with some chopped onion and 1 tbsp of butter inside the chicken. Reach gently until the skin of each half of the chicken breast and place 1 tbsp of butter under it.
4. Grease a glass baking dish with 1 tbsp of oil then place the chicken in it and cook it for 2 h 5 min. Baste the chicken with the drippings each 32 min then serve it warm.
5. Enjoy.

Key Lime Glazed Honey Chicken

Prep Time: 15 mins
Total Time: 15 mins

Servings per Recipe: 1
Calories   1311.7
Fat   82.4 g
Cholesterol   340.2 mg
Sodium   328.7 mg
Carbohydrates   58 g
Protein   87.2 g

Ingredients

1 (4 lb) chicken
1 onion, quartered
3 garlic cloves, peeled
1 lime, quartered
1/2 lime, juice of
1 tsp paprika
2 tbsp honey
1 tbsp olive oil
salt and pepper, to taste

Directions

1. Before you do anything set the oven to 400 F.
2. Place the lime quarters with onion and garlic inside the chicken. Massage the oil into the chicken then season it with some salt and pepper.
3. Transfer the chicken to a roasting pan and cook in the oven for 1 h 10 min. Base the chicken with drippings every 35 min.
4. Get a small bowl: Whisk in it the paprika with lime juice and honey to make the glaze. Brush the chicken with the glaze and cook it for 35 min. Serve it warm.
5. Enjoy.

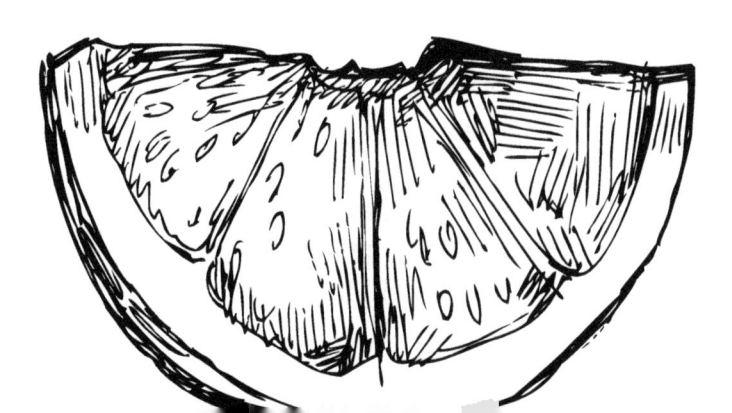

FANCY ROSE'S
Chicken Bake

Prep Time: 25 mins
Total Time: 45 mins

Servings per Recipe: 4
Calories   761.5
Fat   51.9 g
Cholesterol   156.6 mg
Sodium   318.2 mg
Carbohydrates   30.1 g
Protein   36.7 g

Ingredients

1 (2 1/2 - 3 lb) roasting chickens, Cut Into Pieces
1 C. all-purpose flour
salt & pepper
1 tsp oregano
4 tbsp olive oil
3 garlic cloves, Peeled & Sliced
1/2 C. chopped onion
1 sprig fresh rosemary (about 2 tbsps.) or 2 tsp dried rosemary

1 C. chicken broth
1/2 C. vegetable broth
1 lemon, juice of
3 tbsp unsalted butter, softened
1 tbsp flour
1/4 C. fresh parsley, chopped

Directions

1. Before you do anything set the oven to 400 F.
2. Get small bowl: Mix in it the oregano with flour, a pinch of salt and pepper. Dust the chicken pieces with the flour mix then place them aside.
3. Heat the oil in a large ovenproof skillet over medium high heat. Brown in it the chicken pieces then drain them and place them aside.
4. Remove the remaining oil from the skillet leaving 1 tbsp of it only. Cook in it the onion for 3 min then add the garlic and cook it for another minute.
5. Stir in the broth and sit them to make the sauce and simmer it until it reduces by half. Stir in the broth and cook them until they start boiling.
6. Roughly chop the rosemary and add it to the skillet with the chicken pieces. Using a spoon pour the sauce all over the chicken pieces.
7. Cook the chicken in the oven for 22 min. Drain the chicken pieces and place them aside. Cook the sauce in the skillet until it starts boiling.
8. Stir in the lemon with a pinch of salt and pepper.

9. Get a small bowl: Add to it 1 tbsp of softened butter with 1 tbsp of flour. Stir in the remaining butter into the sauce in the skillet.
10. Discard the rosemary pieces and the flour mix while mixing all the time. Simmer the sauce over low heat until it thickens.
11. Stir in the parsley and serve your roasted chicken with the sauce warm.
12. Enjoy.

BAKED CHICKEN
with Italian Seasoning

🥣 Prep Time: 10 mins
🕒 Total Time: 1 hr 25 mins

Servings per Recipe: 4
Calories   813.8
Fat   58.1 g
Cholesterol   267.4 mg
Sodium   542 mg
Carbohydrates   5.3 g
Protein   63.4 g

Ingredients

2 medium onions, peeled
5 -6 lbs whole chickens
olive oil
1/2 tsp salt
1/2 tsp pepper
1 tsp Italian spices

Directions

1. Before you do anything set the oven to 450 F.
2. Thinly slice the onion. Prepare a roasting pan and place in it a rack then lay the onion on it.
3. Massage the oil into the chicken then season it with the Italian spices, some salt and pepper. Place the chicken on the onion with the breast facing down and cook it for 32 min.
4. Lower the oven heat to 400 min. Flip the chicken and cook it for 47 min. Place the chicken aside to rest for 12 min wrapped up in a piece of foil then serve it warm.
5. Enjoy.

Sweet Apricot Chicken Broth Roast

Prep Time: 10 mins
Total Time: 1 hr 5 mins

Servings per Recipe: 6
Calories   310.2
Fat   15.9 g
Cholesterol   88.1 mg
Sodium   256.3 mg
Carbohydrates 12.3 g
Protein   27.9 g

Ingredients

- 1 1/2 lbs chicken parts
- 1/4 C. apricot preserves
- 2 tbsp chicken broth
- 1 tbsp honey
- 1 tbsp soy sauce
- 1 tbsp olive oil
- 1/4 tsp black pepper
- 1/4 tsp ginger
- 1/4 tsp red pepper flakes
- 2 green onions, chopped

Directions

1. Before you do anything set the oven to 375 F. Season the chicken pieces with some salt and pepper.
2. Place a heavy saucepan over medium heat. Stir into it all the ingredients then bring them to a boil to make the glaze.
3. Place the chicken pieces in a roasting pan and pour the glaze all over them. Roast the chicken pieces in the oven for 54 min then serve them warm.
4. Enjoy.

NUTTY CHICKEN
Curry Roast

Prep Time: 20 mins
Total Time: 1 hr 20 mins

Servings per Recipe: 4
Calories 923
Fat 68.6 g
Cholesterol 281.2 mg
Sodium 505.9 mg
Carbohydrates 2.9 g
Protein 71.1 g

Ingredients

1 1/2 kg chicken
1 C. coconut milk
2 tsp thai green curry paste
2 tbsp fresh ginger, grated
2 tbsp lime juice
2 tsp fish sauce
1 small fresh chili, seeded, sliced
2 tbsp fresh coriander, chopped

Directions

1. Season the chicken with some salt and pepper.
2. Get a small mixing bowl: Add to it the remaining ingredients and mix them well to make the marinade. Coat the whole chicken with the marinade inside and outside.
3. Before you do anything set the oven to 350 F.
4. Place the chicken in a large zip lock bag and seal it then refrigerate it for 1 to 4 h.
5. Place the chicken in a roasting pan and cook it for 1 h 32 min while basting it every once in a while with the drippings. Serve it warm.
6. Enjoy.

Zesty Chicken Bake

Prep Time: 10 mins
Total Time: 55 mins

Servings per Recipe: 2
Calories   172.3
Fat   6.5 g
Cholesterol   75.5 mg
Sodium   137.8 mg
Carbohydrates   1.9 g
Protein   25.4 g

Ingredients

1/2 tbsp olive oil
2 garlic cloves, finely minced
1/2 lemon, zest of
1/2 tbsp lemon juice
2 boneless skinless chicken breasts
fresh ground black pepper
salt
2 tbsp fresh oregano

Directions

1. Before you do anything set the oven to 375 F. Season the chicken with some salt and pepper.
2. Get a small bowl: Mix in it the lemon juice and zest with garlic and oil. Massage the mix into the chicken.
3. Place the chicken in a roasting pan and cook it for 22 min. Sprinkle the herbs all over the chicken and cook it for 27 min. Serve it warm.
4. Enjoy.

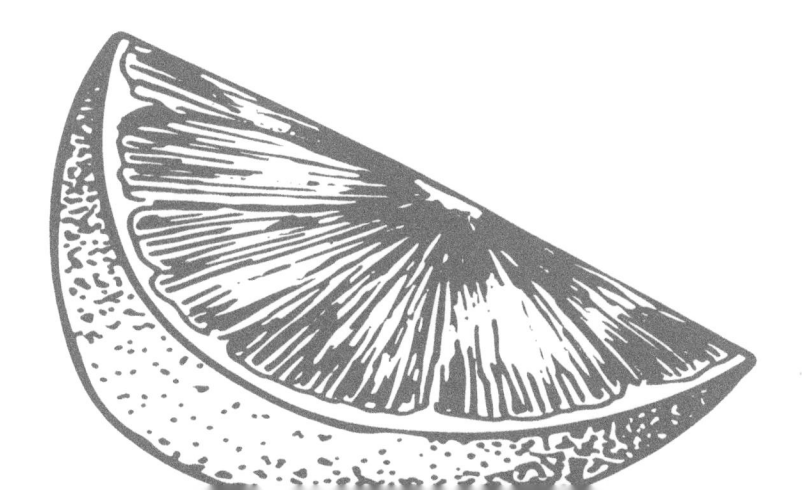

CHICKEN ROAST with Orange Sauce

🥣 Prep Time: 15 mins
🕐 Total Time: 1 hr 35 mins

Servings per Recipe: 1
Calories   2822.1
Fat   209.4 g
Cholesterol   870.6 mg
Sodium   2277.4 mg
Carbohydrates   47 g
Protein   180.5 g

Ingredients

- 1 (3 1/2 lb) roasting chickens
- 1 small sweet onion, sliced
- 1 bunch parsley, with long stems removed
- 1/4 C. butter, sliced
- 1 small orange, peeled and quartered
- 2 garlic cloves
- 1/2 tsp salt
- 1/2 tsp pepper
- 1/4 C. chicken broth
- 1 C. orange juice

Directions

1. Before you do anything set the oven to 350 F.
2. Season the whole chicken with some salt and pepper. Cut the garlic into thin slices. Make several slits in the chicken with a sharp knife and place the garlic slices in it.
3. Place the onion with the rest of the garlic and parsley, butter and orange slices inside the chicken. Tie the chicken legs with a kitchen twine.
4. Cook the chicken in the oven for 1 h 22 min while basting it every once in a while with the drippings.
5. Transfer the chicken drippings into a heavy saucepan and stir into it 3/4 C. of orange juice. Cook while stirring over medium heat until mix becomes thick to make the sauce.
6. Add the remaining orange to the sauce if you need to heat it after it gets cold. Serve your sauce hot with the chicken roast.
7. Enjoy.

Sweet Cinnamon Chicken Roast

Prep Time: 30 mins
Total Time: 1 hr 30 mins

Servings per Recipe: 4
Calories   849
Fat   64.7 g
Cholesterol   243.8 mg
Sodium   1115 mg
Carbohydrates   7.8 g
Protein   58.4 g

Ingredients

- 1 whole chicken, about 4 lb
- 1 cinnamon stick, chopped in pieces
- 8 whole cloves
- 1 tsp cayenne
- 2 tsp cumin seeds
- 1 tsp fennel seed
- 1 tsp coriander seed
- 1 tbsp sweet paprika
- 1 1/2 tsp sea salt
- 1 tsp brown sugar
- sea salt & freshly ground black pepper, to taste
- 1 lemon, halved
- 1/4 bunch fresh cilantro
- 2 garlic cloves
- 3 tbsp extra-virgin olive oil

Directions

1. Before you do anything set the oven to 400 F.
2. Place a large pan over medium heat. Cook in it the cinnamon stick, cloves, cayenne, cumin, fennel, coriander and paprika for 1 min.
3. Transfer the mix to a grinder with salt and brown sugar then grind them. Rub the mix into the chicken from the outside then season its inside with some salt and pepper.
4. Place the garlic with cilantro and lemon halves inside the chicken then transfer it to a broiling pan. Wrap the legs with a kitchen string and cook it for 1 h 5 min.
5. Cover the chicken with a piece of foil and allow it to rest for 12 min then serve it warm.
6. Enjoy.

SKIN STUFFED Roasted Chicken Breasts

Prep Time: 15 mins
Total Time: 50 mins

Servings per Recipe: 4
Calories   137.8
Fat   7.1 g
Cholesterol   46.4 mg
Sodium   236.8 mg
Carbohydrates   1.1 g
Protein   16.4 g

Ingredients

4 chicken breast halves, with skin
8 slices lemons, very thin, seeded
12 leaves fresh sage (can use rubbed sage)
olive oil
4 tsp fresh lemon juice
2 garlic cloves, coarsely chopped
1 C. chicken broth

Directions

1. Before you do anything set the oven to 400 F.
2. Rub the chicken breasts' skin gently reaching under it to make it loose then place under each one 2 slices of lemon 3 sage leaves.
3. Arrange the chicken breasts on a roasting pan dish and pour the oil olive oil them.
4. Pour 1 tsp of lemon juice on each breast then top them with the chopped garlic, a pinch of salt and pepper.
5. Pour 1/2 of the broth on the side of the chicken then cook it in the oven for 27 min. Drain the chicken and place it aside.
6. Transfer the drippings and broth in the pan to a saucepan then add to it the rest of the broth. Cook over medium heat until it starts boiling.
7. Add the garlic from the chicken and mash it then keep cooking it until the broth mix reduces and becomes like a sauce. Serve your chicken breasts with the broth sauce warm.
8. Enjoy.

Bay's Chicken Roast

Prep Time: 45 mins
Total Time: 4 hrs 45 mins

Servings per Recipe: 6
Calories   443.3
Fat   33.8 g
Cholesterol   125.2 mg
Sodium   343.9 mg
Carbohydrates   4 g
Protein   29.4 g

Ingredients

- 1 whole chicken, cut up
- 3 tbsp olive oil
- 1 (8 oz) can tomato sauce
- 1/3 C. balsamic vinegar
- 1/3 C. apple cider
- 1/2 onion, cut in chunks
- 5 cloves garlic, crushed
- 1 tbsp dried parsley
- 6 bay leaves
- 1/8 C. butter

Directions

1. Before you do anything set the oven to 250 F. Grease a baking glass dish with olive oil.
2. Arrange the chicken pieces in the pan with their side with the skin facing up. Divide the butter between the chicken pieces and place on top in the form for dots.
3. Lay a bay leaf under each chicken piece.
4. Get a small bowl! Whisk in it the remaining ingredients and pour them all over the chicken pieces. Cook the chicken roast in the oven for 4 h 55 min.
5. Serve your chicken roast warm.
6. Enjoy.

SOY SAUCE
Chicken Bake

Prep Time: 3 hrs 15 mins
Total Time: 4 hrs 25 mins

Servings per Recipe: 4
Calories   552.4
Fat   38.3 g
Cholesterol   160.4 mg
Sodium   1586.6 mg
Carbohydrates   11.2 g
Protein   39 g

Ingredients

1/2 C. finely chopped lemongrass (3 or 4 stalks)
2 tbsp finely chopped shallots
1 tbsp finely chopped garlic
4 1/2 tsp fish sauce
1 tbsp soy sauce
1 tbsp crushed red pepper flakes
1 1/2 tsp kosher salt
2 tbsp granulated sugar
1 (3 - 4 lb) whole chickens, rinsed and patted dry
2 tbsp finely chopped fresh cilantro
1 tbsp vegetable oil

Directions

1. Get a small mixing bowl: Mix in it 2 tbsp of the lemongrass with all of the shallots, garlic, fish sauce, soy sauce, red pepper flakes, salt, and sugar to make the marinade.
2. Get a large mixing bowl: Toss in it the chicken with the marinade then place it in the fridge for 3 h 3 min.
3. Before you do anything set the oven to 350 F.
4. Remove the chicken from the marinade and place it in a roasting pan. Cook it in the oven with the breast facing down for 42 min.
5. Flip the chicken and cook it 15 to min.
6. Get a small bowl: Mix in it the oil with the remaining lemongrass with cilantro. Spread the mix all over the chicken and cook it until it done.
7. Allow the chicken roast to rest for 12 min then serve it warm.
8. Enjoy.

Basil Baked Chicken

Prep Time: 15 mins
Total Time: 1 hr 30 mins

Servings per Recipe: 4
Calories   1020.4
Fat   60.8 g
Cholesterol   349.6 mg
Sodium   618.9 mg
Carbohydrates   2.4 g
Protein   108.7 g

Ingredients

- 1 (3 1/2 lb) fryer chickens
- 2 tbsp balsamic vinegar
- 2 tbsp olive oil
- 1 tbsp lemon juice
- 1 tsp dried oregano
- 1 tsp dried basil
- 1/2 tsp dried thyme
- 1/2 tsp salt
- 1/2 tsp black pepper
- 1 clove minced garlic

Directions

1. Before you do anything set the oven to 375 F.
2. Get a small bowl: Whisk in it the lemon juice with oil and vinegar. Stir in the remaining ingredients. Massage the mix into the chicken while reaching gently under the skin.
3. Transfer the chicken to a broiling pan with its breast facing up then cook it for 1 h 22 min. Place a piece of foil over the chicken and let it rest for 12 min then serve it warm.
4. Enjoy.

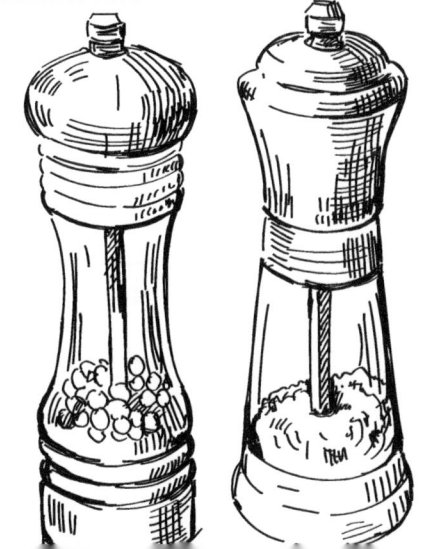

BROWN
Chicken Roast

Prep Time: 15 mins
Total Time: 1 hr 45 mins

Servings per Recipe: 4
Calories   238.8
Fat   15.1 g
Cholesterol   53.5 mg
Sodium   342.3 mg
Carbohydrates   4.8 g
Protein   12.7 g

Ingredients

1 1/2 tbsp fresh lime juice
2 oz chicken broth
1 tbsp brown sugar
1/4 tsp cayenne pepper
1/4 tsp ground cloves
1/2 tsp cinnamon
1/2 tsp dry ground ginger
1 tsp black pepper

1/2 tsp salt
1/2 tsp dried thyme leaves
1 - 3 lb roasting chicken
1 tbsp vegetable oil

Directions

1. Before you do anything set the oven to 325 F.
2. Get a small bowl: Whisk in it the sugar with lime juice and broth then place it aside.
3. Get a small bowl: Add the remaining seasonings and mix them well. Massage the oil into the chicken followed by the seasonings mix.
4. Place the chicken in a broiling pan then cook it for 1 h 32 min while basting it every 25 min with the sugar mix.
5. Serve your broth chicken roast warm.
6. Enjoy.

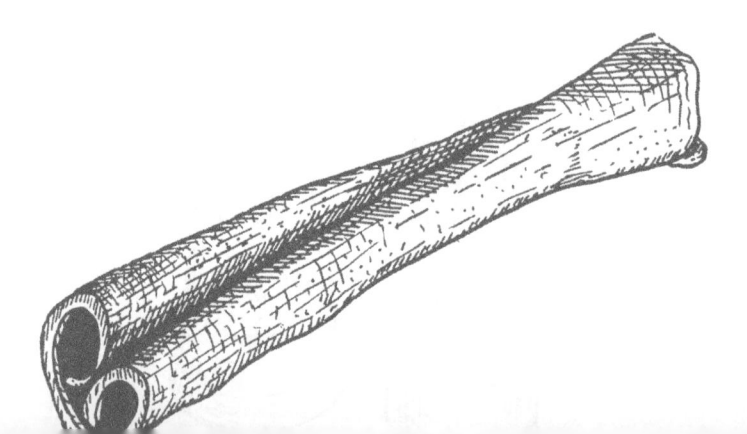

Plantain Chicken Roast

Prep Time: 25 mins
Total Time: 1 hr 5 mins

Servings per Recipe: 6
Calories   541.3
Fat   24 g
Cholesterol   145.3 mg
Sodium   407.3 mg
Carbohydrates   32.9 g
Protein   49.8 g

Ingredients

- 1 tbsp hot paprika or 1 tbsp smoked paprika
- 1 1/2 tsp ground cumin
- 3/4 tsp pepper, fresh ground (divided)
- 1/2 tsp salt
- 3 lbs chicken breasts, and thighs
- 1 tbsp vegetable oil
- 2 large ripe plantains, peeled and sliced
- 6 garlic cloves, sliced
- 3 onions, sliced
- 1/2 C. chicken broth
- 2 limes, quartered

Directions

1. Before you do anything set the oven to 375 F.
2. Get a small bowl: Mix in it the paprika, cumin, the salt and 1/2 tsp of the pepper. Massage the mix into the chicken breasts and thighs while reaching under the skin gently.
3. Place a large dutch oven over medium heat and heat the oil in it. Brown in it the chicken for 4 min on each side. Drain them and place them aside.
4. Add the plantains and cook them for 2 min on each side. Drain them and place them aside.
5. Remove the excess fat from the pot. Stir in the onion with garlic, a pinch of salt and pepper then cook them for 6 min.
6. Stir in the broth and cook them until they start boiling. Place the plantain slices on top followed by the browned chicken then cook it in the oven for 42 min.
7. Serve your chicken roast warm.
8. Enjoy.

SWEET VEGGIES and Chicken Drumsticks Roast

Prep Time: 10 mins
Total Time: 50 mins

Servings per Recipe: 2
Calories 461.5
Fat 13.4 g
Cholesterol 118.3 mg
Sodium 240.1 mg
Carbohydrates 52.3 g
Protein 34.2 g

Ingredients

4 chicken drumsticks (skin removed)
300 g sweet potatoes (cut into chunks)
1 capsicum (red cut into chunks)
1 carrot (large cut into chunks)
1 onion (brown cut into wedges)
1/2 bulb of garlic (wrapped in foil)
cooking spray (Extra Virgin Olive Oil)
1 tbsp oregano (fresh leaves)
1 pinch smoked paprika
fresh ground black pepper
2 large tomatoes (quartered)
1/2 lemon (juice of)
1 tbsp balsamic vinegar
oregano leaves (fresh to serve)

Directions

1. Before you do anything set the oven to 400 F. Cover a baking pan with some baking paper.
2. Arrange on it the chicken drumsticks, sweet potato, capsicum, carrot, onion and garlic. Grease the chicken and veggies with some olive oil cooking spray.
3. Season them with 1 tbsp of oregano leaves, the paprika, some salt and pepper. Cook them in the oven for 22 min.
4. Lay the tomato on the veggies and grease it with some cooking spray. Cook the roast pan in the oven for 19 min.
5. Pour the vinegar with lemon juice all over the roast then serve it warm.
6. Enjoy.

Glazed Honey Veggies and Chicken Roast

Prep Time: 20 mins
Total Time: 1 hr 10 mins

Servings per Recipe: 4
Calories	557.6
Fat	28.4 g
Cholesterol	103.5 mg
Sodium	298.1 mg
Carbohydrates	45.9 g
Protein	31.2 g

Ingredients

- 1 lb potato, scrubbed and cut into wedges
- 2 lbs chicken
- 6 medium carrots, scrubbed and sliced
- 2 tbsp olive oil
- 1 1/2 tbsp honey
- 3 tbsp mustard
- 1 tsp rosemary
- 2 heads garlic
- salt and pepper

Directions

1. Before you do anything set the oven to 425 F.
2. Get a large bowl: Stir in it the carrots with onion, oil, some salt and pepper. Spread the mix on a roasting dish and top them with the garlic
3. Place the rosemary on top followed by the chicken. Cook them in the oven for 32 min.
4. Get a small bowl: Mix in it the mustard with honey. Transfer the chicken to a plate and smother it with the honey mix.
5. Mix the veggies and place the chicken back in the pan. Cook the roast for 18 min then serve it warm.
6. Enjoy.

ROASTED Chicken Pot

Prep Time: 10 mins
Total Time: 10 hrs 10 mins

Servings per Recipe: 6
Calories 812.7
Fat 56.9 g
Cholesterol 283.5 mg
Sodium 264.6 mg
Carbohydrates 0 g
Protein 70.3 g

Ingredients

5 lbs chicken
olive oil flavored cooking spray
seasoning salt
chopped onion
garlic
aluminum foil

Directions

1. Coat the whole chicken with some olive oil then season it with some salt and pepper.
2. Place the onion and garlic inside the chicken. Roll several wads of aluminum foil and shape them into balls then place them in a bottom of a crockpot.
3. Place the chicken on them and put on the lid. Cook the chicken for 10 h 10 min then serve it warm.
4. Enjoy.

Dijon Chicken Roast

🥣 Prep Time: 15 mins
🕐 Total Time: 1 hr 15 mins

Servings per Recipe: 6
Calories   480.4
Fat   35.8 g
Cholesterol   142.6 mg
Sodium   198.7 mg
Carbohydrates   3 g
Protein   34.2 g

Ingredients

1/4 C. balsamic vinegar
2 tbsp Dijon mustard
2 tbsp fresh lemon juice
2 garlic cloves, chopped
2 tbsp olive oil
salt & freshly ground black pepper
1 (4 lb) whole chickens, cut into pieces
1/2 C. low chicken broth

1 tsp lemon, zest of
1 tbsp chopped fresh parsley leaves

Directions

1. Get a small bowl: Mix in it the vinegar, mustard, lemon juice, garlic, olive oil, salt, and pepper to make the marinade.
2. Get a large zip lock bag: Place the chicken pieces in it and pour the marinade all over them. Seal the bag and place it in the fridge for 4 h to an overnight.
3. Before you do anything set the oven to 400 F.
4. Drain the chicken pieces and place them on a roasting pan. Cook them for 1 h 10 min. Drain the chicken pieces and place them aside.
5. Pour the drippings from the pan into a saucepan over medium heat. Stir in the broth cook them until they start boiling to make the sauce.
6. Serve your roasted chicken with the sauce.
7. Enjoy.

SWEET and Tangy Baked Chicken

Prep Time: 10 mins
Total Time: 1 hr 40 mins

Servings per Recipe: 4
Calories 582.2
Fat 35.1 g
Cholesterol 160.4 mg
Sodium 235.1 mg
Carbohydrates 28.7 g
Protein 38.2 g

Ingredients

1 (3 lb) whole chickens
6 tbsp lemon juice, freshly squeezed
6 tbsp honey
2 tbsp tangy grainy mustard
2 tbsp fresh rosemary, chopped

Directions

1. Before you do anything set the oven to 350 F.
2. Get a small bowl: Whisk in it the lemon juice with honey and mustard. Microwave the mix until is heated through and mix it well. Stir in the rosemary to make the sauce.
3. Coat the chicken with the sauce from both the inside and outside then pour the remaining of it inside the chicken.
4. Season the chicken with some salt and pepper. Place it in a roasting pan and cover it with a piece of foil. Cook it for 47 min.
5. Discard the foil and cook the chicken for 1 h 25 min to 1 h 35 min. Serve your roast warm.
6. Enjoy.

Baked Tahini Hummus

Prep Time: 5 mins
Total Time: 1 hr 5 mins

Servings per Recipe: 14
Calories   91.1
Fat   5.3 g
Cholesterol   0 mg
Sodium   146.2 mg
Carbohydrates   9.3 g
Protein   2.2 g

Ingredients

2 C. canned chick-peas or 2 C. cooked chickpeas
2 tbsp tahini
4 tbsp olive oil
1/4 C. warm water
1 large head of garlic
1 lemon, juice of
1/4 tsp sea salt

Directions

1. Before you do anything set the oven to 375 F.
2. Remove the top of the head of the garlic and place it on a baking tray. Drizzle he olive oil on it and then cover it tightly with a piece of foil.
3. Cook it in the oven for 1 h 10 min. Discard the foil and allow the garlic to cool down then remove its skin.
4. Get a food processor: Add to it the roasted garlic with the rinsed chickpeas and the rest of the ingredients then bend them smooth while adding more oil of the mix is too thick.
5. Serve your hummus and enjoy.

JAMAICAN
Wings Roast

Prep Time: 25 mins
Total Time: 10 hrs 25 mins

Servings per Recipe: 8
Calories   230 kcal
Carbohydrates   4.4 g
Cholesterol   48 mg
Fat   16.4 g
Protein   16 g
Sodium   647 mg

Ingredients

3 tbsps Jamaican jerk seasoning blend, recipe in appendix
3 tbsps vegetable oil
3 cloves garlic, diced
1 (1 inch) piece peeled fresh ginger, diced
1 bunch green onions, chopped
12 slices pickled jalapeno peppers
4 lbs chicken wings

Directions

1. Get your blender and mix the following until smooth and even: jalapeno pieces, jerk seasoning, onions, oil, ginger, and garlic.
2. Coat wings with this sauce. Cover the container of wings and sauce. Put everything in the fridge throughout the night.
3. Bake wings in 300 degree preheated oven for 2 hrs.
4. Enjoy.

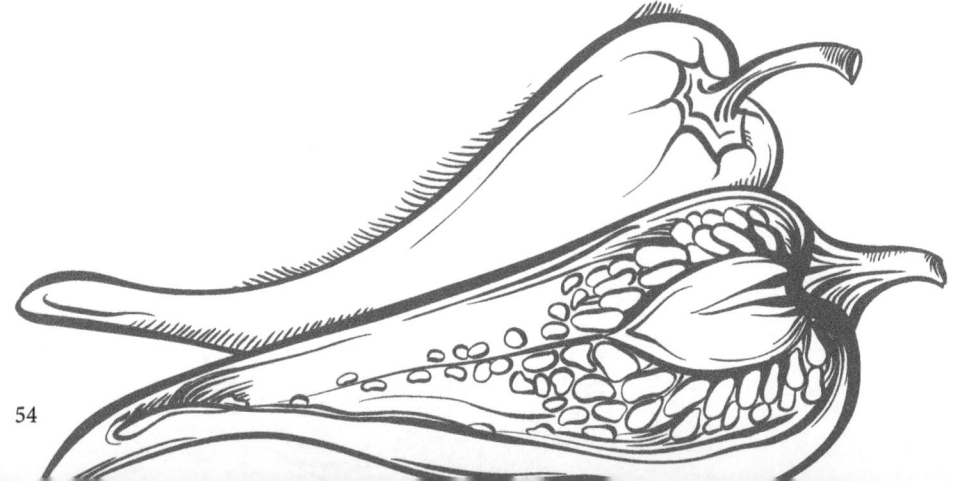

Lightning Source UK Ltd.
Milton Keynes UK
UKHW031125170622
404578UK00008B/1912

9 781975 662455